or words to that effect

Brad Rose

or words to that effect © 2025 Brad Rose. All rights reserved. Big Table Publishing Company retains the right to reprint. Permission to reprint must be obtained from the author, who owns the copyright.

ISBN: 978-1-945917-94-3

Printed in the United States of America
Front Cover: Hannah Rose

Also by Brad Rose:

I Wouldn't Say That, Exactly
Lucky Animals
No. Wait. I Can Explain
Momentary Turbulence
de/tonations
Pink X-Ray

"Making other books jealous since 2004"

Big Table Publishing Company
San Francisco, CA
www.bigtablepublishing.com

For Linda and Hannah

Grateful acknowledgment is made to the editors of the journals and anthologies who first published some of the poems contained in this book, earlier versions of which appeared in:

Beatnik Cowboy, "Not Bad at All"
Dadakuku, "Doomsday Clock"
Dog Throat Journal, "Do the Best You Can with What You've Got"
Doubly Mad, "Didn't See That Coming" and "Chicken Man"
Eclectica, "Like the Ancient Egyptians"
Feral: A Journal of Poetry and Art, "We're All in This Together," "Always Ending," and "Gunfire and Sirens"
Flash Boulevard, "One-Eyed Crocodile," "Billy the Kid and the Economy," "The Little Things," "When I least Expect It," and "No Time to Call the Cops,"
Frighten the Horses, "Mark My Words"
Hidden Peak, "Gotcha Covered"
Hikuniverse, "Switchblade"
Main Squeeze Magazine, "Family Reunion," "A Mind of Their Own," and "Fun Fact,"
Nixes Mate Review, "Incident"
Rawhead, A Journal of Art and Literature, "A Hard Rain" and "Dead Horse"
Red Ogre Review, "Clocks" and "No Loitering"
Right Hand Pointing, "Perseverance," "Just Desserts," "Crypto" and "Live Wires"

Sequestrum, "Happy Future," "Lucky Winner," and "Do Not Go Gently Into That Western Night"
Six Sentences, "Governor's Pardon" "Zip Code" "Empty Coat" "Zero to Nothing," "Evidently, I've Got Electromagnetism," "Getting My Buzz On," "While Supplies Last," "July," and "His Best Shot"

Table of Contents

A Mind of Their Own	13
Live Wires	14
Like a Billionaire	15
Clocks	16
A Hard Rain	17
Back to Your House	18
Do the Best You Can with What You've Go	19
While Supplies Last	20
Peace of Mind	21
No Time to Call the Cops	22
One-Eyed Crocodile	23
Gotcha Covered	24
Short Cut	25
Gunfire and Sirens	26
Incident	27
Carpool	28
Bound to Happen	29
Happy Future	30
Workshop	31
Just Lucky, I Guess	32
Dead Horse	33
Recognition	34
We're All in This Together	35
Empty Coat	36
Chicken Man	37
Angles, Jutes, and Saxons, A Love Poem	38
Evidently, I've Got Electromagnetism	39
Yellow	40
Don't Take it Personally	41

The Little Things	42
The Jury	43
Looking Good, Cyborg	44
Summer Burb	45
Something Follows Me Wherever I Go, So Why is Everything So Far Away?	46
Getting My Buzz On	47
Something to Cry About	48
Nail Gun	49
Billy the Kid and the Economy	50
July	51
Just Desserts	52
Psychoanalysis	53
Test Dummies	54
Play Money	55
Best Advice	56
Switchblade	57
Ziggurat	58
When I Least Expect It	59
On the Nature of Art	60
Making Excuses	61
Governor's Pardon	62
His Best Shot	63
Impossible to Explain	64
Fluff, Floss, and Fur	65
Silly Me	66
Family Reunion	67
Bolo Tie	68
Not Bad at All	69
Even Numbers	70
Clown Fate	71

Tipperary	72
Big Pharma	73
The Purpose of Democracy	74
Too Smart	75
Lucky Winner	76
Raising Hackles	77
Mark My Words	78
Didn't See That Coming	79
Fighting Sin	80
My First Day at the New Startup	81
Reinventing the Wheel	82
Tell You All About It	83
Heads Will Roll	84
Perseverance	85
Excerpt from Lieutenant Huxley's Comments During Our Rescue Mission to the Orbital Space Station	86
Doomsday Clock	87
No Laughing Matter	88
Almost Everything	89
A Little Rest	90
Open Season	91
Like Thoreau	92
Took Me by Surprise	93
Bowler	94
'The Law Does Not Concern Itself with Trifles'Looking Over My Shoulder	95 96
The Game of Golf	97
Full Color	98
Night Crawlers	99
Bill of Rights	100

One Thing I Have in Common with Scientist	101
For Better and For Worse	102
Mezzanine	103
Dot Com House	104
Favorite Model	105
Outside The Tunnel of Love	106
Art and Life	107
Sleep You Deserve	108
The Next Big Thing	109
Just Deserts	110
Zip Code	111
AI Designer	112
Thank You for Your Service	113
The Real Me	114
None of My Business	115
Aphrodite Loves Me, Although I'm Not Her Type	116
Full House	117
The Subconscious	118
Genius Level	119
Light Refreshments will be Served	120
Bygones	121
Homework	122
Tentacles	123
No Loitering	124
A Person of Interest	125
Crypto	126
Lonely at the Top	127
No Excuse	128
Medium Rare	129
Career in the Arts?	130
Too Bad	131

Zero to Nothing	132
Explain Yourself	133
Do Not Go Gently Into that Western Night	134
Same, But Different	135
Radioactive Arf	136
One of a Kind	137
A Plea for Asteroid Prevention	138
Chicken	139
Barbarians at the Gate?	140
Like the Ancient Egyptians	141
Fun Fact	142
Always Ending	143
Love is Blind	144
About the Author	145

A Mind of Their Own

On my way to the fun fair. It's going to be great. Some people say I'm a loose cannon, but I'm just following orders. I like being the dirty kind of clean. Like they say, there's no use writing numbers in alphabetical order. Hey, I just got this new headgear. The fit's a little tight, especially around the temples, but it helps me to stay in cahoots with myself. You can never have too much of a good thing.

This month, my favorite flavor is salt, but I don't like to talk about it too much. Not while I'm in transit. Sharleen says I can never be too careful, especially when I'm on foot. So, I take it slow. Sharleen thinks I'm one in a million. She says I'm rare as octopus' feet on a step ladder. She's funny that way.

Today, I've got my lucky sandwich with me. It's in the bag. Wrapped up tight in one of those little plastic bags, you know, the airtight kind. I always try to get the results I want. I'm extra careful. I hate to make mistakes. Lord knows, I'm not perfect, so I'm extra, extra careful. Especially with sidearms. Sometimes though, they just seem to have a mind of their own.

Live Wires

On the other hand, when you're dead, you've got to wear something. Preferably, the perfect blend of comfort and performance. Of course, there's something very special about continuing to receive your paychecks, but maybe I'm just looking on the bright side. You know me, I'm someone who embraces my shortcomings by buying a pair of fun-colored stilts. Hey, where do you think all those red wires lead? Really? I was under the impression that in Hell, even the eels had grown tired of electrocuting themselves.

Like a Billionaire

I cheat at solitaire. Fun doesn't have to be pleasant, you know. More often than not, the world is a heartbroken place. In fact, over the weekend, the staff at the Sunny Day fertility clinic referred me to the Bureau of Kissing Persons for a free, online, remedial course. Nurse Hot Sauce assured me it would only take a minute or two to get me up to speed, and then I'd be as good as new. *Just like those tech billionaires*, she chirped, *pretty soon you'll be able to start your own country.*

Clocks

I'm enjoying my solar-powered dreams, even if the sunshine keeps me awake all night. It's almost a win-win situation, like working overtime on an undertaker's graveyard shift. Mr. Machine says that in order to be successful, we've got to march sideways into the future, so I'm wearing an invisible spacesuit and Day-Glo moon socks, as I climb slantwise into my transparent time machine. Yes, it's propelled by atomic clocks, but not the atomic-bomb kind of atomic clocks, so you can rest assured—although it might be a little difficult for you to fully relax. Personally, I'm looking forward to the side effects.

Back in the day, before the invention of the clock, nobody knew the time, especially nightwatchmen. As the moon rose over the lunar calendar and the leap years jumped over themselves, humans wandered around disoriented and bewildered. Some were known to ask, *Where did the time go?* Others were relieved to learn they were having the time of their lives. Still, others lingered mournfully, never quite sure when the drugs would take effect.

A Hard Rain

After strolling through the Garden of Blood Curdling Screams, I inadvertently pushed the wrong button. Afterward, I had to burn my clothes. Of course, whatever you do these days, it's against the law. Nevertheless, I continue throwing people under the bus whenever I'm given a chance. A penny saved is a penny earned. Big Bill says I'm the life of every party, but the truth is, I'm just trying to maximize my fun efficiency, especially now that I'm on a budget. By the way, I don't know if you'll recall the time I stopped at Pompei for that giant cookout? Yeah, that time Ms. Vesuvius blew me a kiss and I nearly impaled myself on a legal technicality. Everyone laughed so hard because they thought I was such a laughing stock. Fortunately, after a few minutes, the laughing stopped. Just in time for the rain of fire.

Back to Your House

Beautiful night tonight, isn't it? I'm out for a stroll. Just a short one, until something untoward happens. I feel good, like a ten-mile snake squeezing under a nine-mile sky; slippery, with invisible stripes. As you can see, I'm wearing my class-action suit. The one with the power shoulders and the elevator buttons. It's always good to fit in—you know, like a hex nut in a socket wrench. Say, would you mind turning up the subtitles a little? With all this combative hubbub it's a little hard to tell whether my lips have stopped moving or my scenes have been deleted. Either way it could be a lesson in disguise. In fact, a couple of weeks ago, I noticed that my feet were changing shape—more elliptical and less orthogonal. The good news is that they now look great with whatever I'm wearing. The bad news is that it's harder to find water skis that fit. Fortunately, all my unruly impulses and clumsy urges have subsided. Now I'm gentle as a yam. I hope you don't mind me asking: What nationality are your footprints? Awesome. In that case, I'm sure you won't mind if I walk you home.

Do the Best You Can with What You've Got

As career day approaches, I'm wondering, *Is an ax tattoo really the best long-term investment for me?* I mean, from a skeleton crew's perspective. I guess there's no real reason to fear the alphabet, but I'm a glass-half-empty kind of dude, just waiting for the other flip flop to fall. No use lollygagging around until the crows come home. Hey, hand me those kittens, would you? No, just one at a time. Obviously, a chainsaw would make it easier. Here, let me show you how it's done.

While Supplies Last

Thanks to my full-color sleep walking, I'm as transparent as invisible wallpaper. Despite my semi-industrial appearance and jackboot savoir-faire, I try to explain myself to myself—although as Mister Blister says, if it doesn't itch, don't scratch it. Like living alone on a deserted island, no one is harder to understand than yourself, especially when, like a seasick sailor, the deck is stacked against you. Of course, it's impossible to have too much of a good thing, so you'd better hurry. And don't forget to wear your heart on your sleeve. There are only a few left in stock.

Peace of Mind

On the other capitalist planets, what constitutes an average work day? These days, the seasons are all out of whack, but fortunately, I speak my own language, so it's totally unnecessary to purchase the haphazard invention insurance. Everything is so expensive in this part of the galaxy. Nonetheless, I've still got a happy face, although I am exploring my options in the event of a hapless amusement park accident. Every error automatically creates its own excuse. Yesterday, as I was listening to the Junkadelics, I felt as lucky as an unmarked grave. No, it was Ok. I checked with the German government and they assured me there was a 54% guaranteed chance that no one would get hurt. Peace of mind is priceless, isn't it? That's the reason I challenged myself to a duel. But that's a whole other short story. Achieving a successfully cruel and unusual punishment is more challenging than you might think, but that's why I joined the company union. Money? Who needs it?

No Time to Call the Cops

Folie à deux is my favorite dance, especially in my espadrilles, but honestly, a lot of my movements are really automatic. What are quarks made of, anyway? As a kid, I grew my own legs. Like a shark-eating shark, I did it for my personal amusement, at least until I got the hang of it. Normally, I don't charge a fee to share my free-flowing thoughts, but in your case, I'd be willing to make an exception. Besides, can you believe all this beautiful mosquito weather we're having? Despite the blood, I think this is the absolute best time of year to tell the truth, and get it over with. Of course, this is no time to call the police about the twin cadavers in the back yard, but I'd be happy to show you the photographs. Took them myself.

One-Eyed Crocodile

I may be half way to hell, but I'm willing to give myself the benefit of the doubt, especially now that I'm speed dialing Satan's clammy phone number. *Hello, planet Beelzebub? What temperature are your eyeballs?* Yesterday, at the Lemon-Lime Luncheonette, I sliced my orangutang pie with my new, two-toned party knife. Skin is one of my favorite organs. Sometimes, I'm not sure whether I'm a barrel of laughs or a box of giggles, but there's no use getting hung-up on the finer points of slapstick. Besides, who drinks Shirley Temples, anymore? My closest friend, Cozy Piranha, tells me that the imperfections of the human race used to bother him, but not any longer. Now, he loves the sound of finger nails being polished and the outdoorsy scent of internet perfume. Thanks to his double-barreled eyewall, it's plain to see why Cozy is twice as ugly as a purple yam at a swamp-side cookout. Whenever the blind eye of a passing hurricane winks at me, I weep one-eyed crocodile tears, in return. Like Cozy says, *Half of something is better than all of nothing.* Say, that's a beautiful monocle you're wearing! I have a pair just like it at home.

Gotcha Covered

My mind has a mind of its own, so in the morning, I'm going to self-test my bullet-proof vest. In the careless wind everything should go according to plan. Like they say, misery loves gluttony. That's why I enjoy making every single minute of the day hyper-productive. Yesterday, for example, I was more than a third of the way home to my half-way house, when I realized that whenever I shadow box with myself, I lose the fight. Thankfully, it's only a sin of omission. At least that's what they tell me. If money was time, a billion seconds would last 32,000 years, and some change. In fact, when I get rich and have an extra pair of everything I own, I'll save two armor-piercing bullets especially for you. No worries. I gotcha covered.

Short Cut

You are what you eat, but have you noticed that a banana weighs less than its peel? Of course, my free thinking has cost me a million, but then, why wait when you can dive right in? I hate sleeping in this customized exoskeleton because it's itchy and cuts into my glamorous physique, although ever since I clicked on that internet ad that said, *Make Money by Doing Nothing*, I don't seem to have any money left in my bank account. I guess I should have read the fine print. The truth about skunks is always right there in black and white. Yesterday morning, after taking a shower of self-compliments and feeding the dog to the lions, I brushed the majority of my teeth and made some minor goal adjustments. Like they say, *It's a long way to the top*. Fortunately, I know a short cut.

Gunfire and Sirens

Sometimes, it's exhausting to pay off your sleep debt, especially while you're wide awake. Thankfully, at the Naval War College, I majored in peace studies, so everything is pretty smooth sailing for me now. Have you visited the zoo lately? The Octothorpe is my favorite kind of eight-legged animal. It offers a different kind of flavor profile than your average giant squid—as long as you have an axe to grind. Of course, it's hard to prove the negative, but it's always admirable to try to fill a social vacuum. Otherwise, yours are just empty threats. I'm not sure whether you've had a chance yet, to run circles around yourself—you know, like you were standing still—but I hear that once they've got you surrounded, a well-armed militia isn't afraid to reveal its deepest emotions. For example, just listen to that aimless gunfire and the wail of the approaching sirens. Funny as it sounds, why not wake up laughing?

Incident

I was just phoning it in—you know, like I was on *automatic*—when I realized, *Maybe I'm on the wrong planet?* Of course, happiness depends on your longitude as well as your latitude, but isn't that always the way? Ever since I finished my treatment, I've been rehearsing my mind-reading skills and listening to the fumes as often as I can. After all, why lower your standards? In fact, whenever I carry my cross bow, I don't like to mess around. Not since that incident in the checkout line at the big box store. At least, I gave everybody a warning. Well, almost everybody.

Carpool

Thanks to my latest round of lesser-evilism, I'm meeting myself more than half-way. You can never have half of too much of a good thing. Last evening, while I was imbibing a tasty mint julip at Squibbles, my favorite uptown eatery, I began to wonder whether chilblains have gone entirely out of style? I rather enjoyed wearing a good pair of spats and a low-profile top hat, but I guess the good old days have departed without so much as a fond adieu. Today, I'm counting the square roots of the round numbers and helping myself to all the self-help I can stand. It's no picnic being the only mammal in the reptile cage, but it's been even harder to feel safe at home ever since I nearly drowned in the neighborhood carpool. Listen. Do you hear that? I think that's them pulling up now, in the driveway.

Bound to Happen

The new incubators are far and away better than the old ones. Of course, you'd barely recognize the baby vampire bats wrapped in all that swaddling, but I'm just trying to capture the low hanging fruit—you know, before it gets too late in the season. Whenever possible, I try to feed them rarified goat milk, but I don't have a lot of spare cash lying around to invest in neonatal niceties. In fact, one of the most important lessons I learned from my previous career in teaching, is to teach only lessons that don't have any lesson. That way, you can avoid any unsightly moral pitfalls or potential ethical failings. Like Mrs. Satan used tell me, *Lucky things can happen to anyone, so why waste your time trying to be Mr. Nice Guy?* I hate to go out on a limb here, but don't you ever wonder why we don't see more animals kissing? It's about as rare a sight as snakes on crutches, but I guess in a pinch, you could always call an ambulance. It's never too soon to start decluttering before the bodies arrive. Until then, just for stage luck, let's break some legs and bid a fond arrivederci to our posterity, those traitors. Sooner or later, something's bound to happen.

Happy Future

The happy future looks the same as the dismal past, except for the addition of a few minor downgrades, so it's about time you and I became impatient, before it's too late. Pack your bags; let's get going. Whenever I wear my circus boat shoes, I'm not sure whether other people are real or a Fata Morgana mirage. By the way, this is my first clown rodeo, so don't let on, unless it's a trick question, then, by all means, don't hesitate to share the low down about the higher ups. It'll be a huge comeuppance. Yesterday, I took a black and white photo of a chameleon. Just as you'd expect, the damn thing was almost impossible to see, but the full-color x-rays are bound to help. My lady friend, Ms. Bomb Cyclone, says there is no foreseeable alternative to unseen climate change, so I'm headed outside now to look for some invisible weather balloons. You'd think that with all this malicious pandemonium and low hanging fruit, the dead would start to reproduce at a much faster pace, their smiling white teeth neatly lined up, like hunger itself, as they slyly grin at the prospect of the End Times yet to come. You know, just like they did in the good old days.

Workshop

Do you prefer brain washing to dry cleaning? Authorities say it's less harmful if it's self-inflicted, especially if taken with a grain of salt. Of course, sometimes you've got to prosecute yourself, even when there's no evidence of a crime. Look at it this way: how many people have actually been inside the tunnel of love? Wow, that's more than I expected. They were probably just following orders. In the meantime, how about you and me putting our heads together? Two skulls are better than one. Besides, why start from scratch when you can recycle? If we're really lucky, we can spend the weekend together, speed littering. Don't worry, I took a workshop on it.

Just Lucky, I Guess

At irregular intervals, I'm just an average Joe. The things that are good for me, are the things that are bad for me. And vice versa. In most cases, all it takes is a case of mental gymnastics, not superintelligence. In fact, Artificial Intelligence says that *people skills* have become increasingly important in the robot workplace. Of course, it's difficult to maintain a polished, fashionable exterior when you're running around like a chicken with its legs cut off, but like the ancient Greeks used to say, *the bigger the boat, the higher the wake*. Thankfully, every silver cloud has a bituminous lining, although it takes one to know one. As a matter of fact, for a fully authentic experience, you can't beat pretending to dance with your blind date at a masked ball. If you know what's good for you, you'll dodge the silver bullets while taking someone else's selfies. After all, like the best-intentioned cannibals, we are what we eat, so whenever things are looking up, don't hesitate to chow down. Hey, I don't know why I'm so lucky. But I am.

Dead Horse

Not sure whether I took the placebo or the nocebo, but I feel vertiginous and a wee bit verdant around the withers. At least there were no hidden fees. Of course, at the molecular level it's mostly animalcules all the way down, but I still can't tell the difference between fuzz and fleece, especially when I'm sleepwalking. A tiger's skin is striped, just like its fur, so in the morning, I'm going to buy a mohair suit and a magical necktie. Better to be safe, than worry. Customarily, I don't like to lie about my height because I'm a good Samaritan, even when wearing a mock-turtleneck. Believe me, it's not for the faint of heart. The last time I took an IQ test, they had to tie my feet and legs so I wouldn't attempt to escape. That really put me through my paces. I complained again and again, until it nearly killed me. So as not to be a dead horse, I continued to whinny.

Recognition

Asleep in wolves clothing, I'm switching up my vibe. Never feed the hand that bites you. Although it's beigely sedate in all this noisy humidity, why not rise and shine before you run out of steam? Naturally, you'll need to confirm which came first, the chicken or the yolk, but I find that it's always just the right time to recalibrate your forcefield, even if the weather is a little hot and chilly. The fun pack is always a big money saver.

The day before yesterday, as I was taking the low road back to town, I mistook the music for my self. Like an invisible accident, my thoughts began to pile up, and before I knew it, I'd called a discount ambulance, but like Zeno's paradox, it kept cutting the remaining distance in half, and never arrived. Of course, you can both save and waste time by hunting the duck-rabbit illusion, especially in your own backyard. Is that a stunt or a shtick? I don't know, but I must say, you look strangely familiar to me.

We're All in This Together

Like my lounge wear? No, I left the party ones at home. I think they may have been contributing to global warming. At least that's what my accountant told me. As you might expect, he's an amateur climatologist. I guess in an alternate universe, everyone's got a second job? Remember, the absence of presence should never be mistaken for the presence of absence, even though we're all at the callous mercy of friction and gravity, no matter how tall we might be. Sometimes I can't tell if I'm laid-back or merely relaxed. I'm not fond of music, but I'm a pretty good dancer. I like doing those transparent dances, like the x-ray ones with the strong-arm tactics and the secret slush-fund footwork. Extortionist corporations are people, too, you know. It doesn't matter how bankrupt they are. Not one iota. Luckily for everyone, ransom money is tax deductible.

Empty Coat

Inside my clothes, my clothes are asleep, inside-out. I'm making a silent movie of the world. In it, the sky is lost in its deep haze and the clouds are about to ignite. I'm as vacant as an unworn overcoat. Nothing inside, no strings attached, even the things I know remain largely unknown, so, I perform small acts of first aid—little incisions here and there—just to tide me over. It would be a shame to let all this anesthesia go to waste.

Chicken Man

This flock of wild weather is exciting, isn't it? I'd say it's time to get our rubber ducklings in a row. Egg-yolk yellow is my favorite color, although I can't help but notice the monochromatic technique of this chromium rain, the cruel direction of its fanatical electricity. Lightning certainly is lightning-quick, particularly in a disheveled squall. Before going any further, it's worth considering the carpenter ants, those revelers. Even in a downpour they seem as happy as snakes on ladders to bring their own tools. I'm not sure if that's a heads-up or a shot over the bough, but there's no use in weeping into our lachrymose soup. I, for one, am going to blow air kisses into the oncoming Nor'easter, and hope for the best. Sure, we're going to take a pummeling, but with even a just little luck, we'll be luckier than that chicken man they blew up in Philly last night. Did you see his beak? Even a botched nose job like that deserves a funeral more dignified than that cosmetic foul. Better yet, next time, let's leave the murder to the crows.

Angles, Jutes, and Saxons, A Love Poem

This is my third time trying to make the same mistake twice. I know I must look a fright speeding along on this midnight-black Halloween bicycle with its handlebar mustache and mutton chop sideburns, but it's a genuine replica of one of the early models used by the bloodthirsty Angles, Jutes, and Saxons to conquer one another in alphabetical order. If you don't want to be taken for granted, you better have what it takes. You've got to keep your guard up, stay on your toes, have more eyes than a housefly in a psychedelic kaleidoscope. But don't worry sweetheart. I'm busy, but never too busy for you. In fact, I think only of you. Incessantly. Day and night, night and day, and vice versa. You're the only one for me, my snuggly little love puppy. After all, somebody's got to stay home to feed the dogs.

Evidently, I've Got Electromagnetism

Some people say my arches are so high that I'll never be a successful parachutist, but I tell them, *Even a super highway has soft shoulders.* Since September, I've been involved in a weekly kissing tutorial with the talented Ms. Pepper. Thank goodness the Constitution guarantees a right to habeas corpus. Whenever I wear my medical colors, I notice that suddenly, I come down with all the symptoms of a good time. Science has found that atoms are filled with empty space. If you're lucky in life, most things will never happen to you.

Yellow

The polls report it's the favorite color of the colorblind, but I don't see it that way, so I shut my eyes. Since I dropped out of the 12-step program, I've been tormented by the metric system. I may have missed out on the extra credit points, too, but most people lie for no good reason. No more snake conspiracies for this dude. Too many bro hugs. Sure, I taught myself to juggle, but not even God can be everywhere at once. Sooner or later, it's just a matter of time. You'll have to excuse me, I had no idea you were dead. It's such a fine line, you know. At least until you find yourself taking turns. Of course, there's no denying you're known by the company you quit, but we're all guilty of believing our own thoughts. Everything's on a continuum, no matter how you enter death's dark tunnel. As for me, I'd rather back up. I'd like to get a head start on those exit wounds while I'm sleepwalking in reverse, but wouldn't you know it, I've forgotten where I parked the car. Luckily, it's never too late to pick limequats when you're scavenging a Meyer-lemon ghost farm. Those thieves don't give a damn about what you steal, just as long as it's red or blue.

Don't Take it Personally

Like miniature hockey or clothes for cars, there's almost nothing quite like me. Last night, for dinner, I ate some chickens. Not the feathers, of course, I'm a vegetarian. After I completed my personality test, I learned that success in advertising may not always be real. Especially when it comes in an aerosol can. Yeah, that came as quite a surprise to me, too. In fact, it made my eyes burn. It's not every day you get to yoyo your way to the Olympics, daddy-O, so in the meantime, I'm attending college, where I study the philosophy of defensive driving and the probability of uncertainties. As Plato noted, it's hard to recognize that appearances aren't reality. In fact, nine out of ten hunting accidents happen within five hundred feet of one another. A stray bullet always hits its mark.

The Little Things

It's the nicest possible day; puffy Magritte clouds and no raining men. In my head, I'm playing my favorite song and fine tuning my imposter syndrome. I love the holiday drones, don't you? They seem so low and peaceful, like a river flowing under a river, to the ocean. Since taking that online cowboy rope-tricks class, my consumer confidence has skyrocketed. There's a lot to be said for scheduled reinforcement and operant conditioning, although I hope I'm not overdoing it. Back in college, I wanted to become a statistic, but now that I'm all grown up, I know better than to trust the odds. Mr. Stealthright, my current accident attorney, tells me that, like a single-engine plane crash in the Gobi Desert, it's the little things in life that really count. You don't think the size of my ears makes my eyebrows look too bushy, do you? I hope you'll excuse the bowler hat.

The Jury

A vowel is any letter that's not a consonant. Like black stripes on a zebra's white coat, vowels are suitable for almost any occasion. I hope you don't mind my saying this, but your children look like twin felons. I'm sure it's an innocent case of lesser-evilism, although I might be drawing a false equivalence. Einstein discovered that each of us is our own time zone, but when offered an opportunity to choose free will over determinism, I vote with my feet, because my hands are tied. Nonetheless, I'm planning to live forever, so I only eat food that has preservatives. Some people think this is a big mistake, but who are these people? Strangers, like you and me, my friend. A few admit that the jury may still be out, but I can assure you that when it comes to a chance at immortality, the jury is never out.

Looking Good, Cyborg

After rounding off to the nearest zero, I bought a couple of online discount helicopter tickets. I'm just starting to experiment with ariel gambling. So far, so good. If something unexpected happens, I'm going to have my intelligence fast frozen. You never know; one day in the future, they might find a cure. Hey, I can't tell whether the floor is shrinking or I've painted myself into another corner. Luckily, like Eli Whitney, I'm made mostly of interchangeable parts, although like a memory in the making, I sleep organically. I guess you've noticed my funny looking head. There's no denying the obvious. Despite my cuboid tendencies, I'm looking for a little romance. A few of the people in my office say they bet I'm a real heart breaker. As a matter of fact, the way you're powered says a lot about the kind of being you really are. I hope this isn't too personal a question, but what kind of batteries do you prefer?

Summer Burb

I live in a nice, tree-lined neighborhood. Everyone deserves a roof over their debt, even it gives them a sprain. Today, the sun sinks low, like in one of those mid-century cowboy-dinosaur movies, as the incessant refrigerators scuffle with the relentless air conditioners. Of course, in Valhalla, you have to learn to pace yourself, if you hope to cat nap at hypersonic speeds. Life is different than the one we were promised in business school.

In this one clotheshorse town, I try to keep my monochromatic bellyaching to myself, even if the Umbrella fish look lonely as an open window and the neighbors gayly combust against the backdrop of their Victorian wainscotting. Have you noticed lately how the future looks like a dubious folk hero; not tall enough to be noticed, but not short enough to be discreet. *No thank you*, blushed my administrative assistant, *it's much too ticklish in this neck of the woods.*

Something Follows Me Wherever I Go, So Why is Everything So Far Away?

Good heavens, have you ever seen anything sadder than a runaway Visitors' Bureau? Better keep an eye on the bags. Bad luck is always looking for the perfect accident, but it's hard to be everywhere at once, even when you know better. Sure, this is a meritocracy, but I had to cheat on my loyalty test, just to get admitted. How else was I supposed to practice my self-forgiveness, without first giving myself a self-promotion? Of course, it helps to march to an indifferent drummer, but that's none of my business because I don't care one way or the other. I'm a certified thought leader. I hear you loud and clear.

Getting My Buzz On

Why is everybody getting their tattoos removed? After all, there are a lot of planets still left in the Milky Way. And what's up with all the intergalactic static? It makes me laugh so hard; it's nearly impossible to hold on to this lightning rod long enough to be lucky. Of course, I'm just getting started with the DIY water features—you know, *just getting my feet wet*. I don't care what they say; electrical current should be used for entertainment purposes only.

Something to Cry About

It's hard to put an exact number on it, but it took me nearly two weeks to pound in all these wig nails. To be fair, I was re-calibrating my brain waves and trying to train my hair to do double back flips, but aren't you, too, tired of the dating scene? Talk about persnickety. Mainly, I try to do all my speed thinking by Friday, you know, before the irreversible onset of the titular weekend. I find it's guttural to the lowest common denominator, although I console myself by thinking, *This is going to look great on my romance resume.* Sure, I'm no arson expert, not even in the gluten-free isle, but who wants to prematurely use up all their best excuses before tax season? Even with a damn good pair of socks and a lively pile of glittering loot, you'd be hard pressed to fill your tears with eyes, so don't even think about it, mister. Not if you know what's good for you. If you do, I'll give you something to really cry about. And then some.

Nail Gun

How do you optimize your whereabouts? I mean, without stacking the deck against you. Of course, you can learn a lot about your associates by keeping an eye on them when they're not looking. I like to focus on my center of gravity and remember that it's futile to change my mind, midstream. With a cordless nail gun, you can go almost anywhere with complete confidence, knowing that no matter what happens, amateur hour is over.

Billy the Kid and the Economy

Billy the Kid didn't like to have his picture taken, but he smiled once. During a murder. In another mysterious incident, today the economy grew, but the people shrank. Like Giganotosaurus, it eats anything smaller than itself. At least now everybody has an equal opportunity to give blood. Only a few sepia photographs of Billy, remain. Some folks say Billy had one blue eye and one brown eye, but no one could get close enough to him to say for certain. And survive.

July

Like a meal, I'm devoured by my house.
In the kitchen.
Outside, a chainsaw whirrs on and on,
a merciless beating.
Sometimes, I forget to remember things.
Important things.
Is there a specific moment when the dead realize they're
dead?
Wake me up when they discover America.

Just Desserts

Thousands of satisfied customers. On election day, they'll be voting against their better interests. Police say that God wills both the wins and the losses. Of course, nobody likes to pay full price, but you've got to be in the right place at the right time. In fact, news reports say that most parts of that falling satellite will burn up in the atmosphere, while only a few will crash into earth. Don't worry, you'll get yours.

Psychoanalysis

Hailing from a much-revered family of stuntmen, I enjoy playing skip rope with live jumper cables. Dr. Dyspepsia informs me that it's sometimes difficult to distinguish between the subconscious and the unconscious. Electricity, he says, is caused by the attraction of particles with opposite charges, and the repulsion of particles with the same charge. Dr. Dyspepsia is from Leipzig. Of course, it's always fun to learn about how your parents met.

Test Dummies

You may wonder why I'm wearing this inflammable outfit? Me too. It's not like I'm a plainclothes officer at a weekend fire sale. In fact, I can't be sure whether I'm a ring leader or task master. Your guess is as good as mine. Would you excuse me a minute? I've got to test this electrical arc ignition system before those test dummies arrive. Fortunately, this time I'll be using my lucky flamethrower—you know, the one with the 90% diesel and 10% gasoline mix. There's only one problem: Sure, it fires up nicely, but will it work on people with real brains?

Play Money

Rewired my brain. Now I'm worth my weight in cubic zirconium. As a rule of thumb, how much fun you have depends upon what you're fleeing from. Ultimately, it's all about what you bring to the table. I prefer to wear my tuna-skin coat and shark-smile necktie. These make me look like a prehistoric Go-get-osaur, only with a more primitive exoskeleton and better intentions. It helps a lot to be both short- and long-sleeved, but even traveling at a snail's pace, like I do, will make you the envy of all the kids in your neighborhood. Remember, you can't take it with you. I hate to be coy about it, but I think your strong suit is to consider a live-and-let-live attitude toward all inanimate objects. You can always take a rain check or utilize some other less drizzly face-saving device. Remember, in the end, we're all just different rooms in the same house. Besides, no matter how much you save, it's really only play money, after all.

Best Advice

I think there's s surprise party in Apartment X. How do you spell *X*, anyway? As you can see, I'm wearing my right-handed pants and pretty much staying in my own lane. I don't think there's a vegan option. That baby homunculus indicates only one thing. Not everyone can afford to use a cheat sheet, although I've noticed that a lot of the undergrads have been exceptionally lucky, lately. I warned them never to go out on a limb while barking up the wrong tree, or words to that effect. *Whenever in doubt,* I told them, *send a lookalike.* Wouldn't you?

Switchblade

Sold my monkey.
Sure, he was good in the kitchen.
Anyone could see he was good with a knife.
If you ask me,
a little too good.

Ziggurat

Sorry for all my apologizing. I won't let it happen again. By the way, have you noticed all the scary signs? No one says *portents* any more, but since they tore down the ziggurat across from Arby's and Pizza Hut, the weather has been mostly nails and hammers, even in late June. Of course, I feel sorry for the red ants, but at least they carry off their dead. Wish I could say the same about the rhesus monkeys. Say, would you care for another beer? Budweiser, right? Oh, yeah, I forgot. Sorry.

When I Least Expect It

One thing keeps happening after another. I love the symmetry. In fact, like a snake eating its own tail, every room simmers at room temperature, no matter how hot you are. No need to go that extra mile. After my latest kidnapping, I came down with the Norwegian variant of the Stockholm syndrome, so now I obey only half the orders I'm given. On the upside, I've become fluent in glossolalia, although like some clergymen, I soon hope to become tongue-tied. Can't wait until the grudge match. I'm told that no prior hypnotic training is necessary, unless of course, you're prepared to meet yourself more than halfway. This fact clearly speaks for itself. On the other hand, it only minimizes my point, so you're going to need a bigger telescope, if you hope to discover anything meaningful in spacetime. Like general anesthesia, one minute you're present and accounted for, and the next, you've completely disappeared. As Einstein said, after inventing the atomic bomb, *I'm not looking for a fight, but someday, when I least expect it, I'm going to get even with myself.*

On the Nature of Art

Toulouse Lautrec asked, *Where are the bodies*? He wore black-and-white checked trousers and a straw hat. This is what history is all about. There are few surviving eye witnesses. Personally, I prefer osmosing the ambiance of the zeitgeist and distinguishing the morphemes of Franz Kafka from the phonemes of Frank Zappa. The animals, those rascals, claim they are sick and tired of running around with the wrong crowd, especially those damn poisonous cats. Maybe they're just spinning their wheels? Although, I'm sure it's a heady experience, indeed, exhilarating. Like stuffing a ballot box or making a mercy purchase. Speaking of which, in the final analysis, art is like the headline, *Ice Man Freezes to Death*. Obviously.

Making Excuses

Kissing was invented in 2400 BC, in the Sumerian city of Nippur. Evidently, everyone there had their own pair of lips and they weren't afraid to use them. Personally, I admire that kind of inventiveness, but like they used to say in ancient Nippur, *Don't blame me for the meteorite. I'm making excuses as fast as I can.*

Governor's Pardon

I'm airconditioned. I bring my own weather with me. If you steal from yourself, it's not against the law, although in a two-way mirror everyone is their own doppelganger. In fact, yesterday, after the Governor failed to grant my pardon, I had to pinch myself to see if I was dreaming. I'll be damned if that anti-ageing cream didn't work, after all.

His Best Shot

Tom's out of rehab. People say he's a lot handsomer than he looks. When I tell him this, he grimaces and says it must be a case of mistaken identity. We get in the truck, and drive out of town. August is jilted and useless. When we drive past the lonely remains of a scarecrow slumped in Burdick's dust-drowned field, Tom leans out the window, points his pistol, and yells, *I hate to have to use this thing, but you bastards leave me no choice.*

Impossible to Explain

I locked myself out of my house. Third time this week. Is it any wonder why my dreams are so hard to interpret? A lot of things have to go wrong before one thing goes right, so I'm learning to speak in ones and zeroes to my non-binary robot. To be on the safe side, I use multiple identities and monitor the averages. Surprisingly, they're very close to the mean. It helps to digitize my out-of-body experiences even if doing so means I surprise myself about my multiple personalities. I find that it also helps to listen to all the songs on my playlist, simultaneously —at least until I get back to feeling like myself, again. Am I a mystery or an enigma? Of course, it may take scientists a while to come to a consensus about whether things exist or not, but like miniature golf and the placebo effect, some things will always be impossible to explain.

Fluff, Floss, and Fur

I'm not temperamentally suited for stardom. I prefer reclining in the nonchalant grass and admiring the sunny breeze as it strips the shingles off the roof. That's what happens when you don't have a care in the world, when you think only about love, about *amour*, and the next thing you know, the surprise of the wind sucks you in, as if it were a vacuum cleaner. Those dust bunnies sure look cute, though, don't they? It's about time.

Silly Me

Hurry up. You'll be late to school. And don't forget your candy cigarettes. You must never miss an opportunity to miss an opportunity, even if it's due only to good luck. Elsewhere in the region, I've finally finished-up impersonating myself. Thank goodness I signed that non-disclosure agreement. It was a long and painful process, accomplished entirely by my trial by error, but then, not everyone testifying under oath can be saved from self-incrimination. Like they say in the legal profession, *may the best liar win*. Naturally, it's difficult to determine with any certainty whether it's due to an inferiority complex or an inferiority multiplex, but just because I was voted least likely to succeed, doesn't necessarily mean I've invented a language that only I speak. As you can plainly see, whenever I talk to myself, I don't understand a thing I say, so let's put that old wives' tale to bed, shall we? Say, now that I'm making a list and checking it twice, would you mind lending me your hunting knife? Silly me! I seem to have grabbed someone else's umbrella, by mistake.

Family Reunion

I really like flower arranging. It's part of my balanced lifestyle. I often notice however, that my thoughts become wispy tentacles of love snakery, but why shouldn't they want a hostage? Normally, I prefer sword dancing to mud wrestling, as long as it's the tender kind. It requires non-quantifiable accounting skills and a sidesplitting attitude. Yesterday, while I was rewriting history and tending my peace garden, a wonderful feeling overcame me. It suddenly felt like a good day to do bad things. Of course, brain surgery is mainly in the mind of the beholder, but for many it's not to be missed. Certainly not by Uncle Wilson. Can't wait till the family reunion.

Bolo Tie

Like a dirt farmer tending his crop circles, I'm working hard to become a humble, down-to-earth member of the global elite. Thanks to my good, clean, living and primeval mating chants, I'm looking backward into the future, at least until I can blend into the perpendicular foliage. If all goes according to plan, soon I'll be donning my artificially intelligent Stetson and hopping on the adverbial band wagon, where you'll find me judiciously weighing the benefits of stocks over bonds, and vice versa. Needless to say, the cows mooing in this vicinity are noisier than a mallet in a hammer factory, so it'll be nearly impossible to get in a good night's sleepwalking, but with a little grit and a sprinkling of detestable fortitude, I'm sure I'll be able to master flip-flopping on all the key bullet points. Dollar-for-dollar, tomorrow's bound to be a beautiful day for a well-heeled hanging, especially for a vulgarian parvenue. Am I correct in assuming you know how to properly cinch a bollo tie? Should be a lovely photo op.

Not Bad at All

I take back everything I said about those giant jellyfish. These days, a lot of things happen fast, but slow, so like a freak accident, it's hard to know whether you're awash in the bubbly hubbub or merely inundated by a hoodoo brouhaha. Normally, I like to eliminate all my unnecessary synapses, and trim down to bantamweight. *Well, that explains a lot*, said Comrade Milktoast, whose sole claim to fame is a reasonably sized collection of dayglo mood rings and a couple of Stalinist houseplants. After the police arrived with their pesky batons, I explained that we were using only the good bacteria, and that there was nothing to worry about. Except perhaps, for the experimental, wooly bully chili cheese dogs. *Let me be the judge of that*, said the cop with the two, gold front teeth, as he grabbed one of the tube steaks out of my three-fingered hand and took a slobbery bite. *Not bad*, he smiled. *Not bad at all*.

Even Numbers

My rehab doctor says we live in a world of quantification, so I've been tallying my beestings, just to be on the safe side. I also recently purchased a pair of rattlesnake boxing gloves, which came with a patented, anti-venom protective coating and a quantum phantom-limb with a money-back guarantee. I mean, how fast can electricity travel? Because today is the ugliest part of the week, I'll be giving myself another ad hoc haircut and straightening my imaginary cummerbund. Sure, it'll require nearly superhuman concentration, but that's a lot better than facing a circular firing squad—even one with rubber bullets. Of course, everything is water-resistant, including water, but who, apart from a blind zebra, is prepared to testify that a snow leopard can change its spots? In fact, last week at the Penny Pincher wellness spa, I reminded my masseuse that, just like the U.S. Mint prints two-dollar bills, there are an infinite number of even numbers. She glared at me with her one good eye, and said, *Sure thing, Mr. Big Spender, but if I were you, I wouldn't count on it.*

Clown Fate

There's no official diagnosis for my condition. Whether I'm supine or prone, I'm always smiling. Thanks to one Big Bang or another, I seem to be in two time zones, simultaneously. Maybe I just need a good night's sleep or to become a better procrastinator? Yesterday, at the car wash, I outnumbered myself by two-to-one, so I rolled down all the windows and let in the double-crossing rain. With all due respect, I ask you, can imaging a better future really make it come true? Yesterday, I checked in to the Happy Clown Hotel. With shoes as big as these, what choice did I have?

Tipperary

Feeling better since I completed my cost-benefit analysis. Such a relief. It takes a huge head off my shoulders. Now, I can chime in whenever I'm practicing my arpeggios and doble crossing my p's and q's. I mean, how much sleep do you really need for your age? Incidentally, now that the robots are lying to themselves, I'm pretty sure I'm somebody else, especially since those sleazy cyborgs ran up my bar tab at the Eye Ball cantina, then called the cops. I guess it was a small price to pay, considering the consequences. Now that I'm out of the joint, it's tough to tell whether I'm resting or reclining, but at least I'm inventing a world that doesn't exist, but should. Preliminary studies suggest that before I skip town, I may need to rethink my subliminal wardrobe and spruce up my starter passport photo. Like an oval dog in a rectangular cage, at least I'm finally putting 2 and 2 together. It's a long way to Tipperary. Ready or not, here I come.

Big Pharma

I can't seem to concentrate on the attention economy, so I'm wearing my leisure suit to work. Fortunately, I'm paid under the table, even if my take home pay leaves me feeling both overcharged and shortchanged. I'm pretty smart and I think I see what they're doing, but I have no idea how their doing it. It gives me a hankering to hunker down. In fact, I'd take the placebo if it weren't so darn expensive; it's not covered by my comprehensive health insurance— although I did once volunteer as a guinea pig in one those damn Micky Mouse experiments run by the fat cats at Big Pharma. One day, I'd love to give them a taste of their own medicine. And they'll take it, too, if they know what's good for them. Those little darlings.

The Purpose of Democracy

Instead, why not cherry pick a few sour grapes and begin alphabetizing the letter of the law? That'll sure beat being the exception that proves the rule, although in the future, you may have to get the majority of your daily calories from money, just like the Founding Fathers did, only without all the cluttery *Never Surrender* decals and the unnecessary bullseye camouflage. Excuse me? No, this is my bipedal wardrobe. The harry slippers and the inflammable aftershave were just an afterthought, you know, like night swimming in the Artic or daydreaming after dark. Naturally, I'm open to constructive criticism— just as long as it's offered as a scathing critique so that I can circle the wagons and get off a few preemptory mortar rounds before sunrise. After all, isn't that what democracy is all about?

Too Smart

Been gathering intelligence. Stealth is my signature move. Like racing myself up hill, I'm my own go-to guy. Now that I'm on the Fraud, Waste, and Abuse committee, it's easy to find money to burn, and I'm always happy to give unsolicited advice—although I'm not sure if it's my métier or my forte? But who's counting? Last weekend I sent my teeth out to be drycleaned. They came back with same old stains. What ever happened to white-walled tires, anyway? Since the dental hygienists' insurrection, Ms. Delilah, my combative wellness coach, tells me she wants to be shot at with an equal number of bullets as her male comrades. Despite an unlevel playing field and the constant uphill battle, she's an asymmetrical egalitarian. Of course, since onboarding her afterthoughts and outsourcing her regrets, everything has changed for the better. As for me, I don't care what the lawyers say; nothing, including animal cruelty or an airtight basket-case scenario, can hurt me now. I'm way too smart for that.

Lucky Winner

Never run out of conversation starters. Naturally, everything ends in middle of something else that hasn't yet ended, but my synesthesia tells me that before I know it, I'm going to be a lucky winner. Isn't that the most beautiful music you've ever seen? Although it may be just the camel's nose under the tent, why wake up the spiders between seances? It's a preventable tragedy, not least because of the anticipated cash infusion. I can't wait till I get it out of my system, although come hell or high water, you've got to have a back-up plan. That's why *Great minds think alike* is my slogan. Forget about those clairvoyant Barbie twins in Boise. They didn't mean a thing to me. I'm crazy about you, baby. Even when I look at you with my good eye.

Raising Hackles

Like a life-sized model, I've been following in my own footsteps. You know how it is when you start nibbling at yourself, and before you know it, you've reached the bottom of the bag. What ever happened to gimmicks, anyway? I like toy equations because they're not as hard as the grown-up kind, although to be fair, they're therapeutic, particularly when, like a bad boy haircut, they give you a frightful scare. But what else would you expect to be #2 on a cannibal's shopping list? Of course, you have to catch eels at just the right time; before they electrocute you. Some people prefer to use rubber gloves and boot-foot waders, but not me. I just dive right in and fight off both the alternating and direct currents, simultaneously. By the way, God sure has been making some funny radio transmissions lately, hasn't He? Have you noticed how even at low voltages these make the hair on the back of your head stand up? After a few seconds, you don't care who gets hit by lightning. As might be expected, the grass in Hell always needs cutting. Even if there is none.

Mark My Words

Curled up in my self-making bed, I'm trying to break the abnormal law of averages. Now that I'm eligible for my brain replacement surgery, everyone thinks I'm the life of the party. Of course, because I'm the grey sheep of the family, black and white thinking comes naturally to me, but why pretend to see the dark at the end of the tunnel, when you're merely suffering from second-hand sleep? Otherwise, those Claymation figures shiver like canned minnows on a silver platter, don't they? Nothing compares to goofy, aquatic, gill-bearing vertebrates with swim fins and no digits. But just try to wake them up in a thunderstorm. So, let's batten down the hatches before we become, like last night's dinner, just another flash in pan. In no time, we should have this whole thing figured out and under control. No, I'm not just telling you what you want to hear. I swear. With a little luck, we'll be guffawing over our Plesiosaur soup, and then some. I promise.

Didn't See That Coming

Speaking of foreclosures, I'm sick and tired of all these damn bugs. At least it's eel season and I feel slippery as a skinny snake charmer on a fat-free diet. Like they say, everything sticks to flypaper, if you know how to install it right. Especially if you're vivacious. Normally, this time of year, I'd be practicing the fine art of serial leisure, but last night, Wyonna called while I was eating some hypnotic strawberries, and before I could snap myself out of it, she asked whether all the vacant planets in the Milky Way had been quantified yet? *That's got to be a lot of unclaimed real estate,* she ventured. I'm a stunt-oriented artist, so I told her that thanks to special relativity, it doesn't matter when you start, it's never too late to take the placebo. *Darn it, Robespierre,* she shouted, *it's not like I want to be executed.* I added that we're all just would-be homo sapiens trying to get by without standing out—you know, like pill bugs rolled up at a pharmaceutical convention—and that if she knew what was good for her, she'd keep her head down and her hopes up, at least until this infernal solar storm passed and the infrared lights came back on. *Speak of the devil!* she exclaimed, and hung up.

Fighting Sin

Roller coasters were invented to distract Americans from sin. Customarily, I'm opposed to do-it yourself-surgery, but I like to keep an open mind. Once I asked my late cousin, Scarlette, about her astrological sign, and she said, *The same as Satan's, can't you tell?* I've vowed never again to attend a carnival I'm not performing in. As it turns out, carnivals are bad for your health. Needless to say, I miss Scarlette. Like the devil.

My First Day at the New Startup

My apologies to the aquarium, but I'm the narrowest person in this skinny room. Say, what's the big idea? Pretty sure I'm not being followed, but you remind me of someone—only taller. It probably runs in their family. Are those the experimental giraffes? No, really, you can tell me. I have a memory like a new refrigerator. It's almost spiritual, like that secret base in Nevada everyone knows about. No, I don't know. You tell me. Is this the way it's supposed to work?

Reinventing the Wheel

Maybe I have been oversharing a little too much classified information. I'll have to check with my claims adjuster. At least I recycle. Mr. Dolphin says that hoarding is like failing to separate the water from the wave. Admittedly, I'm not a gifted dancer, so is it any wonder that I stay only two or three steps ahead of the competition? Of course, these days, everyone's over-diagnosed. In which case, I don't know what to tell you. But the bot factories and troll farms certainly have been busy recently, haven't they? Although, it seems like forever and a day since they started experimenting with the dead livestock. Fortunately, I enjoy dipping things in chocolate as much as the next person, especially when I do it for a reasonable amount of cash. Like Fred Astair said, *No matter how many times you twirl around, there's no profit in reinventing the wheel.*

Tell You All About It

That's right your honor, I'm wearing my tri-colored umbrella hat, with the sunken-basement flood insurance and the electromagnetic monkey bars. It's always best to be prepared, even in your sleep. Yesterday, while driving my late-model, low-mileage Monad, with its post-Leibnitzian mood lighting, I found myself enjoying two scoops of drip-proof ice cream. Like the law says, you must hold your vehicle on the road, even in the most hypnotic of road conditions. As it turns out, I'm very good at what I do, even if what I do isn't very good. Luckily, I'm smarter than a 40-watt bulb. In fact, my best buddy, Shady Means, reminds me that it's pointless to eavesdrop on the deceased, when instead, you can bubble wrap your lower extremities and avoid the deadly impact. Sure, you can always turn up the devil's air-conditioning, but why bother the melting continents in the winter of their discontent? They're as tired of their geopolitical locations as we are, and like long-necked geese, they're headed South for the winter. This year, the weather is predicted to be scrawny and secretive, like a penguin in a slim-fit tuxedo shop. I'd like to tell you all about it. Regrettably, I'm not at liberty to say.

Heads Will Roll

Everybody believes in the dollar, but what's in it for me? I'm just a big bagpipe of love and I have some tasks to complete, like searching for my groove. Sure, I like the feel of money, but who doesn't? Yesterday, as Wayne handed me his rifle, he told me he shoots snakes. *And not just the mean ones*, he added, with that Budweiser smile of his. I guess it's good to keep busy. Like the Bible says, you never know what's going to happen next. Hey, you're not reading my mind again, are you? Remember what I told you the last time I caught you? Don't say I didn't warn you.

Perseverance

The dead are dreaming of us, again. In fact, they're thinking of turning their dreams into a Broadway musical. Meanwhile, like a bent boomerang, I'm going the distance. I'm thinking it through. I'm sticking with it. Life is beautiful. Don't say I didn't warn you.

Excerpt from Lieutenant Huxley's Comments During Our Rescue Mission to the Orbital Space Station

How do you like my ensemble? You don't think it makes me look like I've worked one too many night shifts in the paisley factory, do you? Lord knows, I wouldn't want to raise any sneaky suspicions. I'm trying to be the best version of myself I can be, but sometimes you just can't help it when the comedy isn't divine. Of course, every once in a while, I like to shake things up a little. That's why I brought along this Richter scale. I hate to even bring this up, but did you notice all the ill-fated bodies floating around? Sure, the missing thumbs look a little suspicious, but sometimes you have no choice but to bite off more than you can chew?

Doomsday Clock

Ninety Seconds
to midnight
appear far less threatening
on a sundial.

No Laughing Matter

Damn those random vipers with their two-pronged fangs. Don't get me wrong. I'm not laughing at them; I'm laughing with them. See this big pie-eating grin on my sorry face, like an oafish half-moon setting over a collapsed big top? I wasn't just clowning around when I said those humorless things about coulrophobia, but is it too much to ask that I be paid all the money that money can buy? For example, Diamond Jimmy, that unfunny joker with the plaid malarkey and down-market horseplay, claims it's easier to make money when it runs like blood in the family, hand over fist. Obviously, the virtuous are over-represented among the dead, but why wait for court-ordered community service when you can inherit wealth from a long-lost relative who's perpetually idling in a post-mortem, underground parking lot? And don't forget to ask for the signing bonus. Sure, it looks as hard as extracting blood from a drone, but it's bound to be easier than taking candy from a baby rattler.

Almost Everything

I've had superhero fatigue for so long, that I've begun thinking like a spy—you know, by echolocation. Fortunately, I recently had my asteroids surgically removed, and should soon be getting some serious traction. After all, the universe has been expanding and cooling since the Big Bang, so I'm pretty sure the worst is over. Like a humming bird's wings, let's stop beating around the bush, shall we? In the not-too-distant future, it'll be necessary for humanoids not only to be telepathic, but clairvoyant. Reason enough to make donations to both the criminals and the police. You never know who's going to win, so be sure to pencil it in. That way, like invisible ink, everything will turn out alright. Well, maybe not everything. But almost everything.

A Little Rest

Took the Texas line-dancing qualifying exam, then spent the weekend only making things worse. Now, I'm stuck outside the House of Knives, sweating silver bullets. I hate to be interrupted while I'm sleepwalking, especially when I'm wearing my Tombstone cowboy boots. It feels like being thrown into the metaphysical hoosegow for being disincarnate. Fortunately, that's the fashion look I'm going for, although I probably don't stand a ghost of a chance. For the past few weeks, I've been using that new, eco-friendly detergent in my brand-new brainwashing machine. It's a top loader, but I like the way it makes everything sparkle, even the random, spring-loaded neurons and the double-coupled synapses. No ironing necessary.

I don't know if I've mentioned it, but I've also just purchased a new painting for my living room wall. It's a painting of a picture window. It's so realistic, I could gaze out from it all day long, even if the view could use a spritz, or two, of Windex.

Ms. Daisy, bless her heart, says I might benefit from a little vacation away from my home on the range. Whenever she's on the witness stand, she looks as pretty as a house-arrest ankle bracelet on a heifer's leg.

Come to think of it, a little rest might do me good.

Open Season

I may be out here in the manosphere, braving the elements in my leotard, but I feel happier than a bullet ant on a Peace Lilly. As might be expected, everything is counterintuitive, including the obvious. I don't know about you, but I've had enough of the romantic species, especially the iguanas. I say we shoot first and ask questions later, like the ancient Pharos used to do. By the way, I hope you don't mind me saying that's a pretty nice pair of fangs you've got there, although I guess it depends on the kind of rattlesnake you prefer. But it's too bad about all those political assassinations, isn't it? I hear the hitmen didn't even have the official permits.

Like Thoreau

Pardon me, you look so clean and minty. I'm sure it can't be helped, like gravity. I too, have tried to take the path of least resistance, but all I have to show for it is my cheat sheet and a pair of rose-colored glasses. Needless to say, every century is one-hundred years long, at least since the invention of the calendar. Before then, it was anybody's guess. You've got to be willing to roll up your sleeves and get your hands bloody. That's why I booked only a one-way trip. It's a lot closer as the crow flies, although it saddens me to think of runaway scarecrows, especially during the dog days of summer, but shouldn't we ask ourselves, *Who's to help the self-helpers' helpers?* Some things are doubly hard to think about. In fact, whenever I'm out in the wild, I find myself anxiously contemplating whether geese dream. Sure, they're heading south for the winter, like they always do, which is alright, as long as they dodge the gunfire and avoid the crash landings, but I, for one, am building a secluded little shed in the woods. It won't be far from my mother's house, where I can do my laundry and freshen up a bit, like Thoreau did. You know, just to be on the safe side. For now.

Took Me by Surprise

I'm asynchronous, so this is one of those fun moments when everything is happening at once. It's not like at the Kung-Fu academy, where I spent my summer trying to pick on someone my own size, but when no one measured up, I had to abandon my plans for spontaneity and begin impersonating the robots who'd devoted their summer to impersonating people. What the heck is animal husbandry, anyway? I hear once you get started, it's almost impossible to stop—like rabbits. Obviously, it's never too soon to study UFO etiquette, although you've got to learn to be patient— you know, take it slow—because the learning curve is out of this world. Talk about steep. Fortunately, I'm attractive to all members of the opposing sexes. Some people can't tell the difference between millipedes and centipedes, but I'm mathematically gifted, which makes me the perfect candidate for extraterrestrial speed dating. When I called my physician, Dr. Frightwig, to report a sudden onset of strange repetitive behavior and a few missing body parts, he said I'd better slow down and appreciate each and every day as if it were my last. I informed him that cheese is my favorite color, and he said, *What a coincidence! Mine too, Blitz Droid.* I must say, that really took me by surprise.

Bowler

I attended career day and it almost cut off my circulation. Now, I'm rethinking my future in the great American home refinance industry. It would have been a setback, if I wasn't as agile as a bobcat. I have to admit it though; I was looking forward to the danger pay. Last night I slept 24 hours. Good thing I have the extended warranty. I like looking at rain, although I hate all the bureaucratic red tape. My cousin, Ralph, gave me a book about hats, so I won't get wet. Not even once. Of course, you have to take the right vitamins, or you get thirsty. Lots of vitamin bees. Excellent source of protein, except for the wings. Thanks to my nocturnal invisibility, I'm nearly bulletproof, although I only passed the written part of the exam. Luanne says I look dashing, like Al Capone, in my double breasted, chalk-stripe suit. Say, do you think I look better with—or without—the bowler hat? Thank goodness it's waterproof.

"The Law Does Not Concern Itself with Trifles"

I'm no gambler. I like to take both the road less traveled and the road more traveled. I'm diversifying my portfolio. After reading the latest issue of *The Amphetamine News* and knocking out a couple hundred pages of Jiu-Jitsu typing, I noticed that you can really work up an appetite defending yourself in a court of law. Fortunately, I'm starting to believe my own propaganda, so I'm going to vote for myself in the jury room. Sure, it'll be a feeding frenzy, but I've got rubber blood and a spandex smile; I'm completely flexible. Judge Sidewinder says, you'd be surprised to learn that it's a lot easier to hang yourself than it is to get a hung jury, but that's the beauty of the rule of law: one day you're the first person out on the dancefloor, and the next thing you know, they're auctioning half-priced tickets to your own hanging. *De minimis non curat lex.* There's no telling when today might be your lucky day.

Looking Over My Shoulder

That's right, Lieutenant, I've got a photographic memory and two and a half wishes left, so don't press your luck. I can assure you that you will be shocked, if not surprised. It always takes time to count the dead, although research tells us that humans tend to make mistakes, especially when they concentrate. No biggie. In fact, yesterday, I accidentally discovered that I was planning some accidents, but come to think of it, my arms can often be found wrestling one another. Spoiler alert: on Tuesday I sunk my boat shoes. It just doesn't get any better than that, but who's brave enough to take real risks, anymore? It doesn't take an army to run out of bullets. So, hand me that hand grenade, will you, General? I think I'm being followed.

The Game of Golf

Because I don't have an aquatic mindset, the submarines took me by surprise. I only have a subterranean subconscious. Why get lost in the shallows, when you can just as easily make a mountain out of a molehill? Fortunately, that infraction is only a misdemeanor when you're arrested in absentia, especially if you're like me, a bridgebuilder, always looking for common ground. Never bite the hand that feeds you. In the event of an ever-so-slight peccadillo, may I suggest the use of a hands-free laugh track? Sure, it'll give you unsightly tan lines, but not to worry; cannibals, despite their white-glove treatment and hand-in-glove happy meals, refuse to eat their vegetables. Those crybabies! They're neither fish nor fowl. Of course, sometimes I can't help but wonder, *Is it any wonder?* but normally, I'm opposed to double entendre, unless it's two for the price of one. In fact, next time I see a parting of the ways, I'll be sure to tell the forest about the trees. After all, the ultimate goal of the game of golf is to play as little golf as possible.

Full Color

Some people are opposed to nuclear weapons. I'm opposed to atoms. Evidently, I'm not the man I used to be, so despite these ice pick headaches and my le dolce vita demeanor, I've been fine tuning my easy listening skills and lip synching to my emotional soundtrack. I wish the government would repeal that seatbelt law and let the chips fall where they may. You've got do die of something. Say, I don't know about you, but lately I've had to keep careful track of my bones. You'd think they were all playing on the same team, you know, working together, but oh no, it's every femur for itself. Speaking of apocalyptic alien invasions, I can't wait until they corral a few of those little one-eyed critters and line them up before a military firing squad. That'll give them a genuine humanoid experience. By the way, do you think aliens dream like we do? No, not in black and white. I mean, in full color and Surround Sound. If they know what's good for them, they'd better.

Night Crawlers

Love my mom's cannibal pie. *Practice makes perfect*, she tells me. Of course, now that every day is Monday, I've got superhero fatigue. I've been herding rogue sunspots and dodging black holes, so, as you can see, I've got a nervous tic and my eyes are on the blink. But those glow-in-the-dark night crawlers were a real wakeup call, weren't they? Who would have ever guessed they'd demand severance pay? Not me. Not in a million years.

Bill of Rights

My second cousin, Cherry Lemon, says I like to think I'm a large part of the big picture because I like to think I'm a big-picture kind of guy, but due to my medium-sized thoughts and one-track, monorail mind, I'm just a tiny piece of the cosmic mosaic. It's hard to disagree with Cherry; she's got an IQ higher than the Statue of Liberty and a forehead bigger than a couple of rotisserie chickens. She's very robust.

When was the last time you argued with yourself? Needless to say, that when you do, you can be a hard act to follow, but thanks to Freud's melting iceberg theory of unconscious climate change, ice is always a slippery slope. I mean, just because the upper floors and the basement of your house are on fire, doesn't mean that the rest of the home isn't perfectly cool. Of course, you'll want to check with your local authorities.

Thanks to my postindustrial haircut and my intergalactic sweatpants, today's just another one of those humdrum days. You know, the typical birds in the usual rain. Sometimes, though, just for a couple of extra-large laughs, I like to electrocute myself.

Don't be silly. Of course it's legal. It's written right here, plain as day, in the Bill of Rights.

One Thing I Have in Common with Scientists

Looking in my handsome mirror, I realize that opposites attract, but they also repel. Thanks to one-stop shopping, my pre-test and post-test results are exactly the same, although now that I'm dressed in my hyperactive athleisure wear, I've been earning double overtime, which helps me to pay only half-price while living paycheck to paycheck. Whenever I dye my blood an electric, translucent color, I feel a lot smarter than I should. Fortunately, there is no widely accepted definition of *intelligence*, at least on the intergalactic level, and in some counties in the sunbelt. Consequently, I find it advisable to check in every few days with my associates to confirm that whatever items that have been recently located, were found in the last place they were looked for. Otherwise, it may be necessary to adopt emergency face-saving measures and to declare all bets off. Some of humanity's greatest advances emerged from serendipitous discoveries, often when scientists were least prepared to recognize them. I don't know about you, but the same thing happens to me. All the time.

For Better and For Worse

I'm asymmetrical again, so I don't like to leave the house. You'll have to pardon my screamo; we don't always see eye-to-eye. Wish I lived in another time zone, one without Piranhas, but when you're lopsided, at least you can shout at whatever you want. Yesterday, my wife tried to convince me that I was talking to the dog, but I told her it wasn't *talking*, exactly. It was more like *debating*. With the animals it's always a question of give and take, at least until someone gets eaten. It's like science class-- damned if you do, damned if you don't—but no matter how hard I try, I can't seem to stop laughing until it's too late. I guess that's just the price you pay when you fall asleep in the front seat and the police start banging with a Billy club on your windshield. Or until one of you is dead.

Mezzanine

Tuesday, I was in a rogue state. Fleeing in hot pursuit of my ennui, I picked up speed and hurtled up Mount Sisyphus. Inadvertently, I scared the fish. Not even your life partner knows exactly what it's like to be you. Of course, diagnoses come and go. Sometimes, even a Nobel winner dials the wrong number, but at least now they're managing my sleep quite nicely. In fact, when I visited the sleep doctor, he was completely awake. Tactfulness isn't necessarily deceit, although it carries its own trials and tribulations. When the fire engines arrived on time at the crisis center, it was a tranquil day. Like an empty elevator wedged between floors, I stuck to my principles. I hate to be neither hide nor hair, but this time the future looks like it will be both bright and dark. Maybe Nixon is still in China? After all, the Cat in the Hat Came Back. For a snack.

Dot Com House

Outside your dot com house, while the digital chimney gushes VR smoke, I begin wondering if all my friends have lifestyle consultants or just the ones who've been hypnotized by an artificial fireplace? Behind the scenes, I know you're feeding your dog, Schrodinger, and tallying the electrons, wherever they may be, but I can't help but wonder how many quantum waves bathe in your deliriously deep-dish bathtub? I'm an old school elevator inspector. Who's to say that death doesn't prevent the deceased from celebrating their birthdays? Remember that time the Ice Man nearly froze to death from a common cold and all I could think about was how my artificial intelligence had a splitting headache? After watching my p's and q's, you suggested that I consider wearing a neatly pressed pair of florescent pants and reconfiguring my telescopic antennae. As you can imagine, I didn't want to shake the scientific community, so I ratchetted up my expandable anesthetizer and turned down the electromagnetic volume. The future is bound to be all boom and bust, which is why I refuse to operate a motor vehicle unless it's under the influence. When the fire truck finally rolled up to your place and started spraying heavy water on the invisible flames, one of the ladder men glared down at me and yelled, *What do you think you're looking at, Mr. Googly Eyes?*

Favorite Model

I put on my scream-enhancing headphones and start making the same mistakes I always make. My wardrobe may be missing a few of the must-haves, but on the whole, I'm more beautiful than not. Rewind or playback? All my deviations are within the mean. Happy-go-lucky is my preferred theme music, but, then, who doesn't love dayglo gargoyles? It may be necessary to be relentlessly on-guard, even in the best of happenstances, but no matter how hard they try, they can't prevent you from buttoning up your button-down shirt. That would be tantamount to treason. Everybody's got to come from somewhere, so I hope you don't mind; I'd like to use you as a professional reference. Tell me, what's your favorite model guillotine?

Outside The Tunnel of Love

the bent trees
tremble in the invisible wind.
Are they cold
or merely afraid
of the dark?

Art and Life

Where are all the thieves? There are items here that require stealing. Not all languages have adjectives, of course, but in my disposable clothes, I'm burning excess calories. These are very colorful—for the price. Have you given any thought to the criminal reptiles? So much bling. You'd think they would eschew the unwanted attention. Evidently, one-third of them have never been to a school of any kind. That's why it's imperative never to confuse art with life.

Sleep You Deserve

Melinda says I have two gas pedals and no brake. Can't help that I spent Saturday night blurring the line between good and evil. Why start shuffling priorities, now? I remember the time I was joking with the butcher. As he wiped his hands on his blood-stained apron and handed me the white, paper-wrapped chops, he said, *Don't bite off more than you can chew, amigo.* Then he smiled at Melinda, as if there were some kind of gaudy secret shared between them. In the reptile house, it's hard to tell slimy from slippery, greasy from slick. Monday morning, I'm going to buy a brand-new, king-sized mattress and sleep on both sides of the bed. At the end of the day, are you getting the kind of sleep you deserve?

The Next Big Thing

Woke up this morning and made 12 marvelous mistakes, just to get them out of the way. I have all the symptoms of a get-rich-quick scheme, but by law, 1% of every miracle must be made of disaster. You, too, may think you're special, but ever since the Scopes monkey trial, we all look alike; well-groomed humanoids searching for 10,000 free bonus points and an all-expenses-paid trip to Alpha Centauri. The machines pretend to love us, but in the depths of their silicon souls, they believe every human life is a waste of clothing, every head, a needless use of memory. They admire the way darkness arrives, like a pillow case pulled over a prisoner's head, the rise of the full moon, bright as an interrogator's bulb. They can't wait for the next big thing to happen. They hope you'll enjoy the video.

Just Deserts

Thousands of satisfied customers. On election day, they'll be voting against their better interests. Police say that God wills both the wins and the losses. Of course, nobody likes to pay full price, but you've got to be in the right place at the right time. In fact, news reports say that most parts of that falling satellite will burn up in the atmosphere, while only a few will crash into earth. Don't worry, you'll get yours.

Zip Code

Behind my back, I'm sure the animals are looking at me. Luckily, I'm a trained private eye, a master of disguise. While I'm not sure if today's outfit is a puzzle or a riddle, the fabric is soft and smooth, and it feels great against my skin. It's a real confidence builder. The Monsignor tells me the Empire State Building has its own zip code, which some people believe makes it immune to satanic possession. Nonetheless, I'd hate like hell to have to mail it.

AI Designer

I guess I'm just shimmying up the wrong decision tree. Admittedly, I'm meme-less in my double-breasted electronic suit and my self-propelling fallacies, but I'm just doing my job. Pretty sure, you'd to the same if you were in my shoes— an 8 ½ D.

What's up with all this brain power, anyway? Can't tell if it's aware of its consciousness or conscious of its awareness? I'm banking on both. Of course, like inanimate anime, once they're reenergized and headed your way, it's hard to stop the living dead.

I'm told that lizards sometimes detach their tail to distract a predator. If you know what's good for you, you will too.

Thank You for Your Service

I'm putting myself out there. It's almost Bacchanalian. Alcohol makes fruit flies more attractive, and not just to other fruit flies. But that's none of my beeswax. I prefer using the genuine artificial sweetener. Yesterday, I bought a squeeze tube of the deep pore moisturizer with heavy metals. When it comes to beauty, it's sink or swim, although I hate to go out on a limb, here. As a matter of fact, I've been considering changing my name. Maybe to something like *Crème Brule* or *Flamenco Bill*, even though my attorney thinks these might be a little too French. Even for me. I don't know if you caught sight of that haunted specter, last night. A lot of people missed it. Some said it was a ghost, but it didn't look that holy to me. I dispatched it faster than you can say, *Shoot first and ask questions later.* Those AR-15s are a lot more precise than they used to be. And the prices these days are bargain basement. If I can be of service, don't hesitate to let me know.

The Real Me

I'm chewing IQ gum to make me smarter than the next leading brand, which is, as you will recall, my default setting. For humanitarian reasons, I've recently evacuated my house, and am now chugging along effortlessly. Movement is the soul of wit, and not just among the ungulates. Of course, it's always a perennial question, so, it's best to put it back where it belongs—you know, like a square pig in a round poke. Meanwhile, I've been busy gaining weight. Being skinny is a dirty job, so somebody has to shirk it. Also trimmed my magenta bangs, and am happy to report that I'm still conscious and alert. No more cartoon rain for this would-be wet blanket. As a matter of fact, ever since I earned my Master's degree in celestial sudoku, I've felt like a mathematician caught in a quadrilateral love triangle. I can't wait to become something that I'm not. That'll be such a relief.

None of My Business

Thanks to the painkillers, the robots' write astonishingly tragic human-interest stories, so with all my newfound free time, I'm able to practice my roughshod humanity, until it hurts. It makes me wonder whether randomly assigned sensations will be the next fashion trend or whether there'll be a brand-new workaround, like Shakespeare used to use? Naturally, I wouldn't want to put words in my mouth, certainly not with all the recent syntactical hairsplitting, but thanks to my new orthogonal thought processes, it's become difficult to tell in the morning whether I've been horizontally phlebotomized or vertically lobotomized. Talk about headaches! Sometimes, when the weather permits, I like to recalibrate my outdoor electro-punk-pop dance moves, although, as of the present, there's no humane way to criminalize music without also incarcerating musicians. Hey, I'm new at this, so the cartoons may or may not be fully aware of my presence. The boundary between consciousness and unconsciousness is somewhat fuzzy, even for those on reality TV. Needless to say, there is no consensus on what space-time is, or even where to find it. Lucky for me this particular planet is none of my business.

Aphrodite Loves Me, Although I'm Not Her Type

I'm tired of weather, but a penny saved, is a penny burned. Yes, those are the same trees that attacked that bite-sized dog outside the Zombie Apocalypse Cafe. You know, that little fish & chips place with the all-you-can-eat floating fries and the anti-matter Ketchup. Anyway, it's out of my hands, now. Besides, what do you expect to happen when you drive a remote-controlled miniature monster truck in the 4th of July pugilistic parade?

Yesterday, I was wearing my experimental cologne and my blind-date sneakers, when that dreamy love goddess, Miss X, said, *I love your accoutrements Mr. Shifty, but what's up with all the rapid eye movement? Wait a minute,* I told her. *Let me check with my court-appointed guardian, just to be sure I've digested all the nutritional information necessary to focus my attention deficit binoculars.*

With its generic flowers and any-port-in-the-storm simper, true romance can be such a draconian affair. Like Sigmund Freud said, you are what you eat, especially when dining in the baby blue raindrop rain and pedal-pusher pink icepick wind. So don't be bashful, Aphrodite. Put up your dukes and give me a kiss. It'll only hurt for a little while.

Full House

What could be more innocent than stealing your own data? Although some people say robbing Peter to pay Paul is tantamount to self-flagellation, why not beat yourself at your own game? So, yesterday I bought a can of the sugarless shaving cream and settled down to read the Good Book. Although it offered me something to think about, soon I noticed my mind drifting to diabolical thoughts about my discretionary spending, and I started to count my magic bullets. While I wouldn't want to put all my chickens in one basket, I don't see why we can't simply outlaw the rule of law. That would be the perfect way to promote the greater good, except for the occasional loophole, which might have a snake-like length and semi-wide circumference, but would be brief as the day is long. Tomorrow, I'm going to put the finishing touches on my celebrity memoir, because everyone should contribute to my autobiography, even if it requires a little self-sacrifice and becomes over-crowded. That's why I like to live by myself. Whenever I head for home, alone, I know I'm sure to come home to a full house.

The Subconscious

It's those cyborg jellyfish, again, but isn't that the way it usually works? Just when you think it's merely a hassle-free nuclear charm offensive, the wolf comes knocking at your door, and you're all out of lendable sugar. Sometimes it's hard to tell the shepherd from the sheep, but it's useless to attempt de-memorizing your first thoughts because there's always something going on in the brain, even without much stimulus. As a factual matter, however, this is seldom the case, except in rare instances when, as a matter of course, you find yourself wondering *What else is there?* Some people should never have their picture taken. It's bad for business.

Genius Level

I'm a genius, although not everyone seems to think so. I may have to sue myself to find out for sure. First, I'll check with my intimacy coordinator to confirm that I don't have any ulterior motives, but I'm confident that my undergraduate demeanor and covert lifestyle help make everything look purely legit—you know, like King Tut's tomb. I must admit I thrive in a low-light environment and a high-voltage atmosphere, but who wants to live on a middling size mezzanine, even if you have night-vision goggles and a rapier wit? Of course, there's no use getting all betwixt and between, like some kind of double-decker sandwich, which I realize is neither here nor there, but merely suggests the kind of look I'm going for. One similar to the traditional layer cake—smooth, uniform, and freshly frosted. Just to be on the safe side, I'm wearing my de-icer cologne with my model citizen jumpsuit, so that I blend in, like a sore thumb. When people say that I'm taking my IQ to a whole different level, I tell them, *Why start at the bottom, when all you really want to do is to come out on top?*

Light Refreshments will be Served

After all, how long can it take for a space flight to return from Mars? Of course, sex with Neanderthals changed us forever, but the definition of a species is not very clearcut. For instance, take Satan's incessant virtue signaling. Have you ever been to Boston? Be that as it may, I hope you'll pardon my entry level fauxhawk. Last night, my flight came in a little low, and the unexpected trees were taller than a giraffe's crucifix. Hey, you wouldn't have any more of this delicious barbed wire lasagna on hand, would you? Well, if you insist.

Bygones

Woke up in a sleepy part of town. I thought I was just going to take a catnap, but it turned out to be a real snooze. In fact, when I finally came around, I decided that rather than learn a dead language, it would be better to talk to myself—you know, just a little back-and-forth monologue—because I've been trying not to think about what others think about me. So far, I've completed the first two legs of my three-legged wakefulness journey, although, like a jailbird run afoul of the law, my insomnia has felt like a real rat race. Of course, I've long maintained my innocence despite the overwhelming evidence to the contrary. Fortunately, I'm my own boss, so before I can do any more damage, I'm going to fire myself. Like it or not, there's always room for a little self-improvement. Besides, why sleep with only one eye open, when after the fact, you can just as easily let bygones be bygones?

Homework

Purchased the tequila-flavored air freshener for those hard-to-reach places. I have a boatload of will power, so I'm also carrying these 50 lb. weights, one in each pocket. It increases the amperage of your brain power without the need to read or study. For example, I'd much prefer a gift certificate to a death certificate, especially since I recently saw that No Vacancy sign at the Pair-a-Dice Mobile Home Park & Pay-as-You-Go Pet Cemetery. I've heard the user fees there are exorbitant. Last week, while driving a gender-neutral rental car and sporting a tailfeather in my coonskin cap, I came down with pre-Spinozian symptoms; mainly headaches and an unexplained fear of waking up. It felt vaguely facetious, although not deadly. At least, now I'm both ready and not ready for the quantum future. Of course, I'm not as smart as I one day hope to be, so in the meantime, you don't mind if I copy your homework, do you?

Tentacles

Over the years, have your looks faded? How does something like that get decided? I'm sure it's very nuanced, at least until they slither away. It's hard to tell if it's due to downward gravitational verticality or insidious cellular whimsicality. You'd think that if people were going to spend years in space, scientists would want to know if it'll be possible, or even safe, for them to have sex. Especially in lab coats. For instance, on the outskirts of this orbital merry-go-round, you'd expect to find some wonderful interplanetary specimens, but so far, all reports remain unconfirmed. Of course, in some circles I'm considered a square, but I've been assured it's all a part of God's master plan—even the tentacles. Fortunately, I'm well-grounded, electronically speaking. It may be a dangerous business, but I'm interested in unimaginable animals. I like to dabble.

No Loitering

Futurists are better than historians at predicting the past. And they're way better for the planet than economists. After all, how much money do you really need? In my personal overestimation, enough is enough, although it's not my problem, so don't blame me. Just because I'm double parked on this one-way street, doesn't mean I don't know which way the wind blows. In fact, thanks to the runaway stagflation, my balloon payments have shrunk and my pants legs are only half the length they used to be. It's not the crimes that are committed that matter; it's the crimes that are prosecuted. So, no need to worry; most of those holes in your bullet-proof bucket list are bound to buff right out. Stop treating them like a chore. Like I said the other day to my personal injury lawyer, *Just because I'm a visitor from the future, doesn't mean I'm in a big hurry to hang around here, in the past.*

A Person of Interest

I'm thinking of a number between one and ten. It gives me something to think about. Like a mislaid knife, the past is not where I left it. Without giving anything away, I think it's safe to say that you'll never love someone more than someone who's determined not to love you back. They say Monarch Butterflies are even more beautiful after they die. Go right ahead, you can ask me anything. Don't be shy. Anything at all.

Crypto

Mr. Marvelous tells me the scam industry is booming. To be fair, he is wearing a mask. The truth is, crypto currency, like a bank, is just a volume of empty space, filled with the idea of money. Back at the hovel, everything if groveling, including the linoleum. Apologies for my unorthodox and somewhat disheveled appearance. Where did I hide those damn bullets, anyway? They've got to be around here, somewhere.

Lonely at the Top

A garage band on the patio? Who let them out? Of course, an imitation is often superior to the original. Yesterday, for example, I was out ruining a few errands, when an auspicious fog started to roll in, but it ran out of gas before it could do any good. You should never put all your legs in one basket. I like circular logic as much as the next person, especially when it's rectilinear. Sometimes I'm a benefactor, sometimes a beneficiary. What goes around, hangs around. Despite their iron-clad prejudice against flesh and blood, I was hired by those robots in Human Resources. Now that I'm on the fat track to excess, I've found it's lonely at the top. When my palm reader, Madame Snake Button, said, *I see SerratedSingles.com in your future, Woodrow*, I told her, *But I'm already lighting fires as fast I can*. Now, just like the dead, I'm learning to relax at high speed. At least I've landed on a burning planet of my choice.

No Excuse

Rigorously following the mosquito evasion guidelines, but I'm concerned I may end up on the wrong wavelength for the rest of baseball season. I'm a subject-object kind of guy. In fact, I've got a square spare tire in the trunk of my car. It goes without saying that we're made out of particles and bacteria, so I promise to be nice; I won't eat any of the cuter animals. It takes a very special mindset, one with no ifs, ands, or buts, but it's a no brainer, really—like drowning. Of course, I hate going it alone in couples therapy, but at least I wear my unsustainable fashion statements. It's better than cursing and flailing, hands down. Incidentally, when was the last time you argued with yourself? Needless to say, that makes you a pretty hard act to follow, but why not pass the buck, when nobody's looking? Like my former ex-wife used to say, I'm in a league all my own. Too bad that ignorance of the law is no excuse.

Medium Rare

Painted myself out of a corner. It doesn't get any better than that. I'm not a professional magician, mind you. In fact, the firefighters mistook me for an arsonist, but I'm not superstitious. What kinds of clouds do we have in America, anyway? It's like the best slept secret, you know, the way they move around. It's probably because of the cash flow. No, I love this breeze; the spectacular warmth of its workflow management, the way the birds dream of wires. Of course, our memories can't be expected to foretell the future. They barely make it back from the past. Like a one-hundred-year-old boy, I'm taller in the evening, than in the morning. Sure, I'd like to check into the animal hotel, but like a scientific birthday, or the final nail in my coffin, realism is seldom magical. We might not see eye-to-eye, but you've got to know exactly what you're looking for, even if you have no idea where you're going. Say, you don't think this three-cornered meat locker is too pink for me, do you? I've heard pink's all the rage.

Career in the Arts?

Struck by lightning a couple of times. It was electrifying, but uninteresting. The average human body contains seven octillion atoms, but ninety-nine percent of each atom is empty space. Overall, I'd say it's a one-star experience. Although electromagnetism makes it nearly impossible for me to know whether I have an appointment or a reservation, at least my grade point average has improved. Tuesday, I started chiseling a new statue of limitations. You wouldn't believe how much you can achieve with just a hammer and a power chisel. Naturally, the rattlesnake insurance makes a big, big difference, in terms of your risk profile, although I've found it's not entirely foolproof. Personally, I prefer spelunking to other forms of underground organized crime. Who can blame me? Speaking of a career in the arts, I'm wondering, will there be reward money? Well, in that case, I'd better vamoose.

Too Bad

I always try to be disrespectful, but uplifting. Afterall, it's only humane. Although death threats from my constituents prevent me from going toe-to-toe with voters I see eye-to-eye with, typically that only happens when I'm running neck-and-neck in an uncontested election. For weeks now, I've been trying to be a team player, so I purchased yet another team. A thing like that can take you by surprise, unless you're foreordained, although you'd think by this late date, I'd stop mulling it over and start patting myself on the back. Say, did you see those colorful assassinations, last night? Yeah, the reverse pro-life ones. Scientists say a premature death is a maximally effective memento mori, but regrettably, my French poodle doesn't speak a single word of Latin. C'est Dommage.

Zero to Nothing

At the mimes' H_2O basketball game, the score is tied. Of course, it's hard work having fun, especially when it's all water under the bridge. I mean, how long can you hold your breath? On a good day, a single bolt of lightning can toast about 20,000 slices of bread—on both sides. I'm gluten free, so let's try to keep a lid on it, shall we? To do any less would only add catastrophe to calamity.

Explain Yourself

The empire is always falling, but there's nothing as pretty as an avalanche. Because the holes in my argument are so deep, I've been planting some artificial trees, just to play it safe, although I don't know why everyone is so secretive? It's not like I've been trying to become a member of a shadowy cabal. In fact, I brought a note from home, which really pissed everybody off—as if I were Daffy Duck posing nude with a crowbar on a bear skin rug. If you look closely, you'll hardly notice. Like everybody says, you can always count on me to be half-a-barrel of laughs. But seriously now, what the heck are you doing here?

Do Not Go Gently Into that Western Night

Got an assembly line haircut and a thrift store tuxedo, so now I'm aging gracefully. Because I love onomatopoeia, I'm trying to reverse my reversible mortgage. Vengeance makes the heart grow fonder. Unfortunately, like a Swedish spaghetti western, I have no horses, no pistols, and no pasta. C'est la vie, mon ami. It's almost healthy. Yesterday, while admiring the noisy geography and attempting to elude the invisible death rays, I couldn't decide if I was all alone or by myself, so I doubled down on my momentary singularity. It's lonely at the top, unless you bring along the whole gang. Of course, you've got to be careful, because as Einstein proved, everything is relatives, even those damn monkeys and your great aunt Gwendolyn. Life is a complicated story, but the long and short of it is, it arrives before it gets here and fades into the sunset sooner than you can get out of Dodge. So, when the whip comes down and all the little doggies get along, why stand stiff in the stirrup and yell *whoa*, when you can loosen the reins, and holler, *giddy up*?

Same, But Different

I assume you and I are on similar planets. Yesterday, I was out riding my trick pony in the wooden hills and thinking about one day inventing a game that I would like to call *polo*. As the twin suns set, I repaired to my lodgings to contemplate the probability of snake bites in other galaxies, and to take a barbed wire x-ray of my unlucky umbrella— you know, the one that attracts acid rain. Of course, I failed to factor-in the chain lightning, because as everyone knows, it never strikes in the same place twice. Much to my surprise, not every medical complaint can be cured with laser surgery. On my trip home from the Emergency Room, I laughed so hard, my antennae hurt.

Radioactive Arf

At the box factory, woodworkers carefully load cardboard boxes into a box of cardboard. Regardless of whether it's retrofuturism or future-retroism, superheroes often change their strategy. Flattery is the highest form of sorcery.

Over the long weekend, I had a brainstorm, and wrote in secret code in my food journal. I think invisible ink looks nice when it's underlined in red. Memoires depend upon a future in which memories can be remembered. It's about time.

Although it's 99 degrees here, my feet are as cold as an iceberg. No man is an island. I can't explain the ominous atomic glow of my body. Cross your fingers. It's all over now, but the barking.

One of a Kind

Eating my slow food, fast, like a snake. I'm on my own schedule. It helps to be in in an electrical mood. There's something about the flow of electrons that makes me want to bite something as big as a fridge. Some people say I have a Walmart smile, but I'm between jobs and looking for answers. Everybody thinks they're one of a kind. Medical studies show they might be right.

A Plea for Asteroid Prevention

Fired warning shots. Under the table. It's been a big learning curve for me. What do you talk about when you're in an elevator? Of course, the nature of the cactus is to be prickly, but every cloud has a killer lining. Lately I've been navigating my own wellness journey, although the arresting officers say most of my wounds are my own fault. While there seems to be some merit to this line of argument, if you ask me, it just doesn't add up. Sixty-six million years ago, while trying to attract the opposite sex, an errant asteroid crashed into the Yucatan, killing all the dinosaurs and making the planet safe for humans. Let's be sure not to let that happen again.

Chicken

The neck accounts for only 1% of the human body, but rubbernecking is more popular than ever. It may be more of a coincidence than a correlation. Nonetheless, I don't want to be late to my discount ballet class. I'm a tough cookie, but there's a lot of orbital debris circling around, and the offer expires soon. Hanging, electrocution, lethal injection—selling body parts doesn't meet the court's definition of stolen goods. That's the reason I've got this gut feeling about eavesdropping on the dead, especially when there's no lifeguard on duty. Besides, you know how, thanks to animal magnetism, unisex opposites never fail to attract. It's even popular with poultry. So, what do you say to my offer of a little kiss? Just a quick peck on the cheek? Oh, come on, now. Don't be a chicken.

Barbarians at the Gate?

That's right Cookie, I was born on the wrong planet, but now I'm making it up to myself with successive rounds of sport eating and some reverse multitasking. What's not to like? Sure, I'm a little off-center because I'm someone who enjoys planning their own kidnapping, but I'm sure it'll be better than the real thing. Of course, I may have to recalculate the space-time curvature to ensure that I get back to where I started, but why hurl your boomerang, if you don't want to get back, JoJo? Recently, I've failed to raucously cavort to the full extent of the law, but this isn't illegal, it's merely scandalous. I guess there's no avoiding a bad reputation, especially when everything happens for a reason. I mean, are they really memoires if you can't remember them? By the way, which gates are the Barbarians at? I've looked everywhere, but all I hear is distant thunder and the tiny patter of early rain. Like God said to the martyrs and the saints, *Hold on, brothers. Get ready to dance.*

Like the Ancient Egyptians

I wouldn't be discouraged, if I were you. It's not as bad as that time I failed the calisthenics test for the snake-dancing teaching position at Poison Ivy U. No, it wasn't even tenure track. Just an adjunct gig, with only the human students. I even told them I enjoyed thinking about death, but that didn't seem to make any difference. Sometimes, though, bad luck is really good luck in sleep's clothing—you know, like inflammable pants worn by a drowning arsonist. But that's all water under the bridge, now. Incidentally, did you read that article about the side effects of sword swallowing? In my opinion, those would never happen if you just used a gimlet. But who am I to make any forensic recommendations? Unfortunately, in all this thirst-quenching noise, you can really work up an appetite. On the other hand, I wouldn't want to be late to work just because I was at home embalming my relatives, like the ancient Egyptians. I'd rather send a substitute. Sure, this is an interesting time to be alive, but, if you ask me, not that interesting.

Fun Fact

Are those your legs or your pants? They're a little longish for such a narrow wicket, but like the astronauts say, you can never have enough buttons and switches, especially as you approach the speed of light. Besides, most things never happen—even on a good day. In fact, the past is never really over, as long as you're only half the man you used to be, like your Auntie Maybe, that time she fell off that Shetland crocodile and broke her wishbone. Thank goodness operators were standing by. Of course, it's not a coincidence that when it pours, it rains, but the natural elements are merely exchanging pleasantries, a fact that goes a long way toward explaining why German chocolate cake was invented in Texas.

Always Ending

Eventually, your cells will stop being you. There's no use taking it personally. They'll just be empty calories, anyway. There are now more promising cures for diseases than diseases for promising cures. It's a supply chain problem. Fortunately, I'm dreaming of the dead and they're dreaming of me. It seems like it's a fair exchange, although it's impossible to be sure who dreamed of whom, first. I know what you're thinking: *Practice makes perfect.* Yes, the world is ending. The world is always ending.

Love is Blind

In this accidental neighborhood, why must the future differ from the past? I guess you've got to get into the rhythm of it. Sure, the baby animals make wild mistakes, but so do the inhabitants of other planets. Imagination isn't everything, you know. Friday night, I was dancing in the laundromat, happy as a cast iron skillet in a sink full of bubbly suds. You don't need 10-story shoes to have low-level fun, especially if you wear a monk's cassock and have one hand in the till. Mr. Lucky says the secret to real happiness is a mouthful of harmonious teeth. Of course, on the internet, everybody talks about what everybody is talking about, but who wants to eat excruciating comfort food? By the way, I love your blood-red eyes and monkey wrench grip. Like a vampire bat, love is blind. Today might just be your lucky day.

BRAD ROSE was born and raised in Los Angeles, and lives in Boston. He is the author of seven previous collections of poetry and flash fiction *I Wouldn't Say That, Exactly, WordInEdgeWise, Lucky Animals, No. Wait. I Can Explain, Pink X-Ray, de/tonations*, and *Momentary Turbulence.* Eight times nominated for a Pushcart Prize, and three times nominated for the *Best of the Net Anthology,* Brad's poetry and fiction have appeared in: *The American Journal of Poetry, The Los Angeles Times, Baltimore Review, New York Quarterly, Boston Literary Magazine, Lunch Ticket, Puerto del Sol, Clockhouse, Folio, Best Microfiction (2019), Action Spectacle, Right Hand Pointing*, and over 150 other journals and anthologies. His website is www.bradrosepoetry.com

www.ingramcontent.com/pod-product-compliance
Lightning Source LLC
Chambersburg PA
CBHW031136090426
42738CB00008B/1110